Vicksburg

HENRY HOLT AND COMPANY · NEW YORK

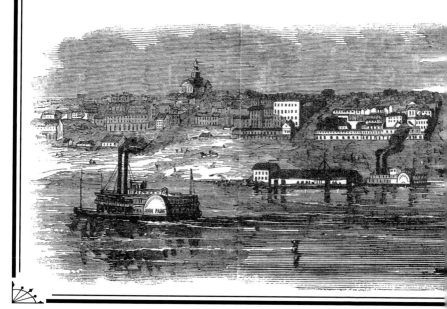

MARY ANN FRASER

Vicksburg

THE BATTLE THAT
WON THE CIVIL WAR

I wish to give special thanks to Gordon Cotton and Jeff Giambone of the Old Court House Museum in Vicksburg, who shared their extensive knowledge about both the campaign and the museum's wonderful collection. I also wish to acknowledge Frank Wood of the Frank and Marie Wood Print Collection and the staff of the following institutions who provided information and photographs: the Library of Congress; the U.S. Military History Institute at Carlisle, Pennsylvania; the National Archives; the Vicksburg National Military Park at Vicksburg, Mississippi; the Chicago Historical Society.

Many of the illustrations in this book were taken from on-the-spot drawings made by artist correspondents during the war for *Harper's Weekly* and *Frank Leslie's Illustrated Newspaper*. The sketches that were made in the field were converted to woodcuts for publication. Like today, people wanted to know what things looked like while they were happening. These two weeklies provided the primary pictorial coverage of the conflict.

Henry Holt and Company, LLC, *Publishers since 1866*
115 West 18th Street, New York, New York 10011

Henry Holt is a registered trademark of Henry Holt and Company, LLC

Library of Congress Cataloging-in-Publication Data
Fraser, Mary Ann.
Vicksburg—the battle that won the Civil War / by Mary Ann Fraser.
p.   cm.
Includes bibliographical references and index.
Summary: Describes the events preceding and during the key Civil War battle of Vicksburg,
its significance, and its aftermath.
1. Vicksburg (Miss.)—History—Siege, 1863—Juvenile literature.
[1. Vicksburg (Miss.)—History—Siege, 1863.   2. United States—History—Civil War, 1861–1865—
Campaigns.]   I. Title.
E475.27.F73   1999   973.7'344—dc21   99-19701

ISBN 0-8050-6106-1 / First Edition—1999
Printed in Mexico

1 3 5 7 9 10 8 6 4 2

To those who died at Vicksburg,
may their courage continue to inspire us.

The Vicksburg National Military Park

Contents

~~~~~~~~

Vicksburg Is the Key   *3*

The Yankees Are Coming!   *13*

On Dry Ground with the Enemy   *31*

Johnny, Keep Your Head Down   *53*

Vicksburg Has Surrendered   *79*

Notes   *90*

Glossary   *95*

Bibliography   *98*

Index   *101*

Vicksburg

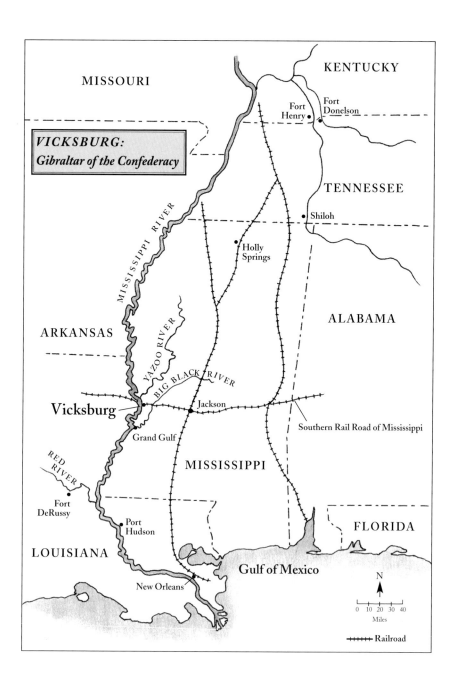

MISSOURI

KENTUCKY

Fort Henry
Fort Donelson

TENNESSEE

VICKSBURG:
Gibraltar of the Confederacy

MISSISSIPPI RIVER

Shiloh

Holly Springs

ARKANSAS

YAZOO RIVER

ALABAMA

BIG BLACK RIVER

Vicksburg

Jackson

Southern Rail Road of Mississippi

Grand Gulf

RED RIVER

MISSISSIPPI

Fort DeRussy

Port Hudson

LOUISIANA

FLORIDA

Gulf of Mexico

New Orleans

N

0 10 20 30 40
Miles

++++++ Railroad

Vicksburg Is the Key

It was mid-November in 1861, only seven months into the American Civil War. President Abraham Lincoln stood before a skeptical audience of Federal officers. He pointed to a city on a large wall map. "Vicksburg is the key," he declared. "The war can never be brought to a close until that key is in our pocket."

A great many Northern politicians and military leaders believed the only way to win the war was to capture the Confederate capital of Richmond, Virginia. President Lincoln disagreed. He had worked as a flatboatman on the Mississippi River and had seen firsthand Vicksburg's importance to the South.

"We may take all the northern parts of the Confederacy and they can still defy us from Vicksburg," he explained to the officers in blue. The Confederacy used the Mississippi River as its lifeblood. The river could easily transport men and arms. Southern cotton, shipped downriver, could buy everything the Confederate army needed. Union control of the Mississippi from its source to the sea would cut off supplies to the Confederacy, hurt the South's economy, and split Louisiana, Arkansas, and Texas from the other Southern states.

By the summer of 1862, Union forces had made great strides toward controlling the Mississippi River. While Federal armies fought their way down from Illinois, Admiral David Farragut sailed his fleet up from the Gulf of Mexico and captured New Orleans. But in the heart of the Mississippi Valley stood the now heavily fortified city of Vicksburg, the center of rebel resistance, the "Gibraltar of the Confederacy."

Steamboats crowd the Vicksburg wharves. *(Photo courtesy of the Library of Congress.)*

Since its early development by the Reverend Newit Vick, a Methodist minister in the early 1800s, Vicksburg, Mississippi, had grown into an important commercial center. Perched beside the "Father of the Waters," its docks served the region that produced most of the nation's cotton. Cotton meant everything to the South. By the outbreak of the Civil War, Vicksburg had become one of the largest cities in the state, with a population of close to 5,000. Corn, cattle and hogs, foreign weapons, and other supplies for the Confederate troops came from the West and South to the port of Vicksburg. From there they were sent east by the Southern Rail Road of Mississippi. This railroad connected to other lines leading to every important point in the South. The Confederacy's own president, Jefferson Davis, had a plantation not twenty miles south of Vicksburg. He believed the city was "the nailhead that held the South's two halves together."

At first the citizens of Vicksburg voted against leaving the Union. But when Mississippi became the second state to secede, they quickly embraced the Southern cause and began raising troops and placing cannon on the bluffs overlooking the river.

The Union navy made its first attempt to capture Vicksburg in late June 1862. After three months of constant bombardment, the city was as strong as ever. The navy could not do it alone.

Meanwhile, in the East, Lincoln was fighting his own political battle to keep the North together. The South's reasons for fighting the war were fairly clear: secede from the Union and protect its way of life, which was based on small farms and on plantations with slave laborers.

In the North, more and more people were working in factories and living in cities. Cheap labor came from new immigrants, not enslaved black Americans. When the war began, the North was not focused on abolishing slavery. Rather, its main purpose was to prevent the South from bringing slavery into new areas, and to reunify the country. Now, more than a year later, many Northerners were ques-

President Abraham Lincoln played a major role in determining the Union's strategies, policies, and troop movements during the war. *(Photo courtesy of the Library of Congress.)*

tioning whether slave states should be held by force. The Civil War had already outlasted most people's expectations. They wanted the bloodshed to end even if it meant the breakup of the United States. The North was not only battling with the South, it was also struggling to define its own goals.

President Lincoln knew that the longer the war continued, the more the North itself would be torn apart. He needed victories—and soon. He needed Vicksburg.

After the navy failed, Lincoln searched for another way to put the Vicksburg key in his pocket. He turned to Major General Ulysses S. Grant. To many people the stocky, brusque, and businesslike Grant was not an obvious choice. Although a graduate of West Point and a veteran of the Mexican War, he was not a smooth, polished leader and tended to wear what was comfortable rather than regulation. But he had a clear way of thinking that cut to the very core of the matter at hand.

In the first year of the war Grant attracted a lot of attention, not all of it good. A clerk in his father's store when the war began, Grant entered the Union army determined to fight for reunification of the states. His victories at Fort Donelson and Fort Henry in February 1862 demonstrated that he was an effective and strong-minded

Major General Ulysses S. Grant, a professional soldier, would become the Union commander in 1864, having demonstrated that he had the military skill and confidence other Union generals lacked. A staff officer once said he wore "an expression as if he had determined to drive his head through a brick wall, and was about to do it." Major General Sherman once exclaimed about Grant, "To me he is a mystery, and I believe he is a mystery to himself."
(Photo courtesy of the U.S. Army Military History Institute.)

commander. The press called him "Unconditional Surrender Grant," playing on his initials and the tough terms he demanded. But jealous enemies rumored that he was insubordinate and often drunk. Although Grant successfully rallied his army from near defeat at Shiloh, his superior, Henry Halleck, was frustrated by Grant's independence and upset by Shiloh's staggering death toll. Halleck and others wanted Grant dismissed. President Lincoln responded, "I can't spare this man. He fights!"

Grant understood that people fighting for a cause would never give up until they lost all hope. If he tried to avoid needless deaths in battle, he would only make the war last longer, killing more people in the end.

On October 25, 1862, Ulysses S. Grant was formally named commander of the Department of the Tennessee, which included everything along the Mississippi south of Cairo, Illinois. Immediately he sent a proposal to Halleck in Washington requesting to move on Vicksburg.

Taking Vicksburg would be no simple task. It stood like a citadel 300 feet above the wide and powerful Mississippi River. A direct attack from the river was considered suicidal. Some forty rebel guns armed the overlooking bluffs. Attacks from land were equally difficult. As one Confederate engineer put it: "After the Lord of creation had made

Lieutenant General John C. Pemberton was an experienced and respected soldier who had the misfortune of facing Grant at the height of his command. *(Photo courtesy of the U.S. Army Military History Institute.)*

all the big mountains and ranges of hills, He had left on His hands a large lot of scraps; these were all dumped at Vicksburg in a waste heap."

For an army to take Vicksburg it would have to first fight its way deep into enemy territory. Then it would have to force its way through the mazelike watery wilderness that surrounded the city to the north and west, unless a general could come up with some totally unexpected means of attack.

President Davis put Lieutenant General John C. Pemberton in charge of Vicksburg's defenses. Forty-eight-year-old Pemberton was a West Point graduate and an experienced soldier. Although capable at discipline and administration, he lacked imagination.

General Joseph E. Johnston was nicknamed the "Gamecock" by his men. A graduate of West Point Military Academy, he was trained in classic military strategy.
(Photo courtesy of the U.S. Army Military History Institute.)

Over Pemberton, Davis then assigned General Joseph E. (Joe) Johnston, one of the South's most respected officers. Serious differences arose immediately between the two commanders. Pemberton believed in defense; he wanted to turn Vicksburg into an impregnable fortress. Johnston wanted to be more aggressive, smashing the Federal armies wherever possible.

Hunker down or attack: Which would save the city—and the South? March through the disease-infested swamps to attack from the north or run the gauntlet past the Vicksburg batteries and approach from the south: Which would allow a constant flow of supplies to the troops, conquer the "Gibraltar of the Confederacy," and bring victory to the North?

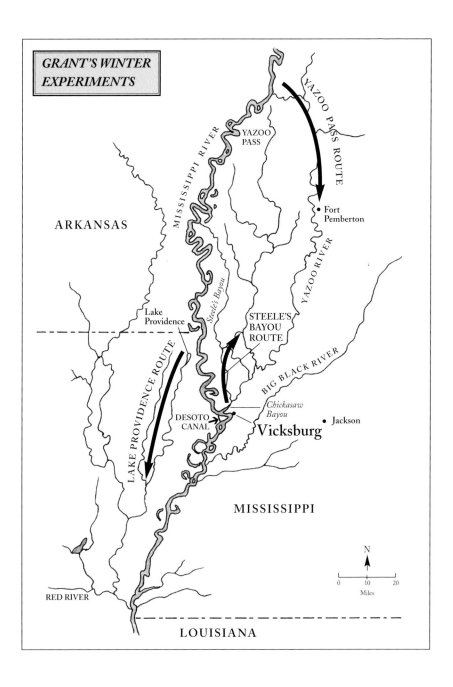

GRANT'S WINTER
EXPERIMENTS

ARKANSAS

MISSISSIPPI RIVER

YAZOO
PASS

YAZOO PASS ROUTE

• Fort
Pemberton

YAZOO RIVER

Steele's Bayou

STEELE'S
BAYOU
ROUTE

Lake
Providence

LAKE PROVIDENCE ROUTE

BIG BLACK RIVER

Chickasaw
Bayou

DESOTO
CANAL

Vicksburg

• Jackson

MISSISSIPPI

N

0   10   20
Miles

RED RIVER

LOUISIANA

The Yankees Are Coming!

In November 1862, word reached Grant that people in Washington within his own department were working against him. For months another Federal commander, Major John McClernand, had also been planning an attack on the port of Vicksburg. McClernand was not only a soldier but also an ambitious politician and a friend of President Lincoln's. Grant later noted in his personal memoirs, "Two commanders on the same field are always one too many, and in this case I did not think the general selected had either the experience or the qualifications to fit him for so important a position. I feared for the safety of the troops entrusted to him."

Halleck made it clear that Grant had total command, but Grant mistrusted the political situation. In an effort to beat McClernand to Vicksburg, he decided to revamp his

Major General John A. McClernand was a successful Illinois politician for many years before the war. He used his military position to seek glory and advance his political ambitions. Fellow commanders, including Grant, found him difficult to work with, and Grant looked for an excuse to get rid of him. *(Photo courtesy of the U.S. Army Military History Institute.)*

initial plans. He would distract the Confederates by moving south from Holly Springs, parallel to the Mississippi River, while maintaining his supply line. At the same time his close friend, and favorite corps commander, William Tecumseh Sherman, would attack from the river at Chickasaw Bayou, northeast of town.

At the time, supply lines were considered a necessity for any large army moving deep into enemy territory. A supply line provides a link to a home base. Without one, troops have to transport all their supplies—food, medicines, munitions, horses, wagons, and spare equipment. A supply line enables a large force to restock as it moves. But Grant's troops would be forging deep into Southern terri-

Major General William Tecumseh Sherman believed in total war. He was one of Grant's most trusted divisional commanders, and although he sometimes questioned Grant's tactics, he remained one of his greatest supporters. *(Photo courtesy of the Library of Congress.)*

tory. They could not easily protect the supplies they left behind.

On December 20, Grant's supply depot was destroyed by rebels. The major general assumed he could not advance as planned and sent his men into the countryside to scrounge for food and equipment. "I was amazed," he later recalled, "at the quantity of supplies the country afforded. It showed that we could have subsisted off the country for two months instead of two weeks." Although Grant lost his supplies, he learned a valuable lesson: He could move without a supply line and live off the land.

When an army is attacking a city, both sides have advantages and disadvantages. The city can defend itself with its walls, guns, and well-planned defenses. But that security also limits movement and the ability to know when and how the enemy will attack. It must rely on spies in the field, pickets, and couriers. The attacking army, meanwhile, can move about and confuse the defenders, but they must carry everything with them or rely on a supply line, which is always vulnerable to raids. The defenders sit and wait; the attackers aim for a surprise assault.

The telegraph, invented by Samuel Morse in 1844, changed the way wars would be fought. During the Civil War, commanders and politicians far away from the fighting could be in instant contact with those on the battlefield. Pickets could alert troops of enemy movements without delay. Such was the case on Christmas Eve in 1862.

Believing that Grant was distracting Pemberton, Sherman continued his drive toward Vicksburg aboard Admiral David Dixon Porter's ships. He was completely unaware that Confederates had planted a secret telegraph wire along the river.

Around midnight a lavish Christmas ball was well under way at the Vicksburg home of William and Emma

Balfour. Across the river at DeSoto Point, a Confederate army telegrapher, Philip H. Fall, suddenly awoke to a series of frantic dots and dashes. The call was coming from a post upriver. "Great God, Phil," the message said, "eighty-one gunboats and transports have passed here tonight." Fall tore into the stormy night, lamp in hand,

Sherman's troops attacking at Chickasaw Bayou.

and rowed across the turbulent river. After running to the Balfours' house, he interrupted the party with the alarming news: The Yankees are coming!

Sherman's troops had delayed along the way. This, together with the dots and dashes of Morse code, gave the Confederates time to collect reinforcements.

When at last the Yanks arrived at Chickasaw Bayou, Sherman tested the Confederates' defenses and ordered an attack. Slogging through the muck left by recent rains, two brigades led the assault. Captain William Olds of the 42nd Ohio Regiment described the scene: "As the storming brigade advanced it found itself in the center of a converging fire, a flaming hell of shot, shell, shrapnel, canister and minié balls. It would be vain to attempt any description of the noise and confusion of that hour."

From the top of the bluffs, rebel fighters fired their guns straight down upon the charging Yanks. In an effort to escape the murderous fire the soldiers of the 4th Iowa Division clawed out burrows in the cliffs in which to hide. The soldiers tucked into the hillside remained in their shallow caves through a driving rain until, at last, darkness descended. One by one they snuck back to their camps.

Federal casualties (the number of people killed, lost, or wounded) were nine times greater than Confederate casualties.

Sherman was not willing to give up so easily. He made plans to attack again from another location five miles away. It was New Year's Eve.

Just as the last preparations were under way, a blanket of fog smothered the battlefield. A torrential rain followed. Watermarks on trees made it clear that if the river flooded, the men would drown. Sherman quickly sent his troops back north. He wrote to his wife, "Well, we have been to Vicksburg and it was too much for us, and we have backed out."

With each Union setback, the antiwar movement in the North gained strength. Back in Washington, President Lincoln was realizing that he needed to establish a clear goal, one that people were willing to fight and die for, or he would lose support for the war. On the morning of New Year's Day, Lincoln quietly retired to his office and signed the Emancipation Proclamation. From that day forward all slaves in rebel states were free in the eyes of the Union. With the signing of the proclamation, the ending of slavery became a central goal of the war. Although opinions regarding slavery

The First Reading of the Emancipation Proclamation Before the Cabinet by President Lincoln, engraving created by Alexander Hay Ritchie. *(Engraving ICHi-11211, courtesy of the Chicago Historical Society.)*

were mixed in the North, emancipation was a strong rallying point that Lincoln viewed as both a moral and a military necessity. But would it be enough to sustain the Union?

On January 3, 1863, John McClernand arrived in Mississippi with orders to take control of Sherman's troops. Grant chose to leave his headquarters and to command field operations himself. By the end of the month he had 60,000 soldiers divided into three corps led by Major Generals William Tecumseh Sherman, John McClernand, and James B. McPherson.

Grant's men were suffering through one of the wettest

winters on record, and he felt it was better to keep them busy than to have them sit out the cold months enduring from disease and low morale. The difficulty of the terrain between the Mississippi and the Yazoo Rivers convinced Grant that Vicksburg could not be challenged from the north. He decided to attack from below the very city that blocked his passage down the river. But how could he get past it? He launched four different projects, each aimed at finding a way to get his men south of Vicksburg via surrounding waterways. Grant would later refer to these four projects as his "experiments."

The first project came at the strong encouragement of President Lincoln. In June of the previous year the navy had dug a shallow, narrow canal across mile-and-a-half-wide DeSoto Point, a peninsula formed by a hairpin turn in the Mississippi River. Lincoln felt DeSoto Canal was worth a second try since it would allow Union boats to move to the south of Vicksburg without having to pass in front of the town's batteries.

Each day a thousand of Sherman's soldiers plus black workers taken from local plantations and drafted into the Union army labored in the quagmire of mud and twisted tree roots. General Grant later recalled, "This long,

Former slaves digging the canal across DeSoto Point.

dreary . . . winter was one of great hardship to all engaged about Vicksburg."

Just as preparations were completed to cut the temporary dam and let the Mississippi flow through the canal, a new torrent of rain dredged it away. Instead of the muddy waters flowing through the canal, they flooded the peninsula and fields, nearly drowning the soldiers. Grant had seen enough. In mid-March he called off the DeSoto Canal project.

Frustrated by the canal's slow progress, Grant had already begun to focus on a new experiment forty miles away. This plan involved cutting the levees (earthworks that kept the river from overflowing) between Lake Providence and other navigable waterways. Large vessels could then steam ahead to a point sixty miles south of Vicksburg, avoiding the guns on Vicksburg's bluffs.

Throughout the sluggish, marshy rivers and streams, called bayous, grew snarls of vines, oak, cottonwood, and giant cypress trees. McPherson's men invented a saw that could cut underwater, but Grant soon realized clearing the waterways might drag on for months. The Lake Providence project was also abandoned.

Winter was nearly over and Grant's army had accom-

The crew of the *Queen of the West* escaped in boats and on floating cotton bales after Confederate guns shot through a steampipe.

plished nothing. Diseases, such as malaria, typhoid, and smallpox, had diminished the troops. The flow of supplies through Vicksburg to Confederate armies continued.

Meanwhile, Admiral Porter decided to deliver a strike of his own. He directed Colonel Charles Rivers Ellet, the nineteen-year-old son of the inventor of the ironclad steamboat, to stop commerce along the Red River, a tributary of the Mississippi. Three tinclads, or metal-plated steamers, led by the *Queen of the West* successfully ran past the batteries of Vicksburg and up the Red River, ramming and torching Confederate ships along the way. At Fort DeRussy, three miles north of Marksville in Louisiana, the *Queen of the West* ran aground and was abandoned.

The Confederates captured the *Queen.* Then they used her to attack the *Indianola,* forcing Ellet to leave her beached a short distance below Vicksburg.

With humor and a dash of ingenuity, Porter devised a scheme to stop the South from salvaging the doomed tin-clad. For the price of $8.63, using barrels for smokestacks and logs for cannon, he decked out a barge to look like a massive gunboat. With pitch fires burning under the

Admiral Porter's dummy gunboat bears down on the rebels salvaging the *Indianola.*

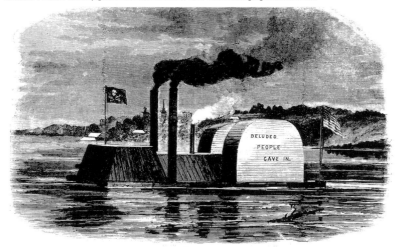

phony smokestacks, the vessel drifted past the Confederates salvaging the *Indianola*. The trick worked. When the Confederates saw the monster warship menacing them, they set fire to the *Indianola* and scurried for safety. The fake warship then plowed into a sandbar. Later, when the Confederates crept close for a better look, they discovered they had been duped. There, on the bow of the ship, was a pirate flag with skull and crossbones and three-foot-high letters that read, "Deluded people cave in!"

The make-believe gunboat was not the only disguise in the Red River campaign. During the Civil War nearly a hundred women pretended to be men in order to become soldiers or spies. One such woman fought for the Union during the Red River campaign. Her real name was Jennie Hodgers, but she had enlisted under the name Albert Cashier. A fellow soldier described her as "the smallest man in the company." She managed to keep up her pretense for many years after the war. Her true identity was not discovered until she was hospitalized following an accident in 1911.

While Porter worked with tinclads and props to halt supplies entering Vicksburg, Grant desperately searched for an alternate route. Years before the war, a system of

A steamboat navigating a bayou, smokestacks pulled back.

waterways to the east of the Mississippi River called the Yazoo Pass had flowed into the Yazoo River. Grant figured that if his troops cut the levee blocking the entrance to the pass, they could follow the old waterways and descend upon Vicksburg from the east.

On February 2, 1863, the Union blew up a section of the levee and the swollen river roared through. Pemberton was on to Grant's plan. Confederates had choked the waterways with debris and had begun construction on a defensive outpost, called Fort Pemberton. Unable to launch an effective attack against the fort, the Union expedition returned to the Mississippi.

Grant's last and most extraordinary attempt to reach Vicksburg began March 14, when Porter's squadron of five tinclads, two mortar boats, and two tugs entered Steele's Bayou. The narrow passageways barely allowed the cumbersome boats to pass. Overhanging tree growth scraped the decks and toppled smokestacks. Debris clogged the waterways. When Porter learned the rebels had sunk a coal barge in his path and that artillerymen were on their way, he knew the expedition was in trouble and sent for Sherman's troops. Just when the situation looked hopeless, Sherman's infantry arrived, marching through the waist-high water and driving off the rebels. Unable to advance or turn around, the two cumbersome gunboats laboriously backed their way out of the swamps.

It was late March. The DeSoto Canal, Lake Providence expedition, Yazoo Pass project, and Steele's Bayou expedition had all failed to deliver the Vicksburg key. Many Yankees had toiled in the mud and now lay buried beneath it, the victims of typhoid, pneumonia, or dysentery. Republicans and Democrats alike labeled Grant an incompetent.

General Cadwallader Washburn wrote to his brother, a main supporter of Grant in Congress, "He is frittering away time and strength to no purpose. The truth must be told even if it hurts. You cannot make a silk purse out of a sow's ear."

The Vicksburg campaign and Grant's career were both in jeopardy.

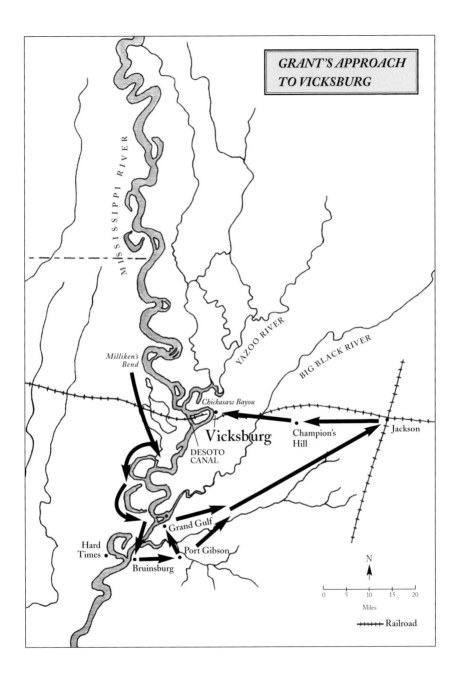

GRANT'S APPROACH
TO VICKSBURG

MISSISSIPPI RIVER

YAZOO RIVER

BIG BLACK RIVER

Milliken's Bend

Chickasaw Bayou

Vicksburg

DESOTO CANAL

Champion's Hill

Jackson

Hard Times

Grand Gulf

Port Gibson

Bruinsburg

N

0   5   10   15   20

Miles

+++++ Railroad

On Dry Ground with the Enemy

⟳⟳⟳

All through the winter, Grant's objective was to get below Vicksburg. He reasoned that if he was to take the city at all, it would be from the one direction no one had thought of—the south. Now that the floods in the countryside were receding, he hoped much of his army could make it there on foot.

The troops were to march down through Louisiana to Grand Gulf, thirty miles below Vicksburg. Admiral Porter would then run steamers and barges loaded with supplies past the batteries of Vicksburg. He could then rendezvous with Grant at Grand Gulf to ferry the troops to the east side of the river. The army and navy would aid General Nathaniel Banks in an attack on Port Hudson, Louisiana, another Confederate stronghold on the river. Banks and Grant could then move on Vicksburg together.

Although Porter agreed to cooperate with Grant, he seriously doubted that his three unarmed river steamers would make it past the batteries. Both Sherman and McPherson also openly opposed this new plan. They pointed out to Grant that he would be outnumbered two to one with no sure means of supplying his army and no route for retreat if defeated. Sherman recommended that they return to Memphis and start over again with a new supply line. Grant refused. "The problem for us was to move forward to a decisive victory, or our cause was lost. No progress was being made in any other field, and we had to go on," he told Sherman.

Grant was going against the advice of the men he knew best and respected most. Colonel William F. Vilas, of the 23rd Wisconsin, observed that "It is an interesting commentary upon its military nature that his warmest friend and ablest general, Sherman . . . endeavored to dissuade him." Yet Grant, like the Confederate commander Robert E. Lee, believed success was not possible without risk, and he was willing to gamble with his career to prove it.

Grant opened his campaign by instructing McClernand to clear the way down through the swamps west of the Mississippi. McPherson's corps would follow. Progress went at a snail's pace. The men had to corduroy the rutted and muddy roads with logs laid side by side. The ground was still too wet for them to bring supply wagons along, so they had to carry everything they needed and hope Porter's supply boats made it past Vicksburg.

About this time Charles Dana, a special commissioner assigned by the secretary of war to spy on Grant, requested permission to travel with the general. Grant realized immediately why Dana had been sent, but agreed to let the commissioner join his army. Dana soon was quite

Troops corduroying roads.

David Dixon Porter first went to sea at the age of ten. He joined the Mexican navy at fourteen and two years later entered the U.S. Navy. After his success at New Orleans he was named admiral in command of the Union's Mississippi Squadron in late 1862. *(Photo courtesy of the U.S. Army Military History Institute.)*

taken by the major general and later reported, "Grant was an uncommon fellow—the most modest, the most disinterested, and the most honest man I ever knew, with a temper nothing could disturb, and a judgment that was judicial in its comprehensiveness and wisdom." This from a person sent to record his faults.

Upriver, Porter prepared the first group of ships for the perilous voyage past the batteries of Vicksburg. To protect the boilers and conceal their fires from the enemy, bales of hay and cotton were stacked all about the decks. Anxious men stood ready with cotton wads and gunny sacks to plug any holes below waterline or to put out fires.

Fortunately for the Union, Grant's bayou expeditions during the first quarter of the year completely misled

Pemberton and Johnston. They believed that a discouraged Grant had given up and was returning to Memphis. The commanders were convinced Grant posed no immediate threat.

At last on April 16, Porter's squadron was ready. "We knew they were to have a grand ball that night in Vicksburg, and thought the sounds of revelry would favor us in getting the transports past the batteries," Porter explained. "The plan decided upon was that the ironclads should pass down in single file, . . . and that when in front of the batteries they should engage them with their broadside guns, making as much smoke as possible, under cover of which the transports should endeavor to pass unseen," a newspaper reporter explained.

At the appointed hour, boats teeming with Yankee spectators gathered on the river to view the operation. At the head of the canal floated the *Von Phul*. It carried not only honeymooners McClernand and his wife but also Grant with his wife and four children who had come down from Memphis for a visit.

With their engines muffled, Porter's vessels cruised around DeSoto Point in the moonless night. Confederate pickets aboard small skiffs sighted the steamers and

The Union fleet passing the Vicksburg batteries. *(Courtesy of American Heritage Engravings.)*

sounded the alarm. Then they bravely crossed the river in front of the enemy to set fire to tar barrels and cotton bales, illuminating the ships for the gunners on the bluffs.

Confederate General Dabney Maury, his wife, and newly christened baby were sound asleep when the action began. At the boom of the first shot, the general awak-

ened, quickly dressed, and bolted out the door to see what was happening. He said, "It was the grandest spectacle of my life. . . . Our batteries were in full play, blazing away at the line of gunboats making their way past them and giving shot for shot."

Mary Loughborough, wife of a Confederate staff

Grant did not like to be separated from his family, who often followed him throughout the war. Here he is, seated, with his wife, Julia, and their four children. Frederick, Grant's eldest son, is standing in the middle. *(Photo courtesy of the Library of Congress.)*

officer, also described the spectacle: "My heart beat quickly as the flashes of light from the portholes seemed facing us. Some of the gentlemen urged the ladies to go down into the cave at the back of the house. . . . While I hesitated . . . a shell exploded near the side of the house. Fear instantly decided me, and I ran."

Downriver aboard the *Von Phul*, Grant's twelve-year-old son, Frederick Dent Grant, saw "The river was lighted up as if by sunlight. . . . My father and I stood side by side on the hurricane deck. He was quietly smoking, but an intense light shone in his eyes."

One by one the vessels shot up their rockets, signaling that they had passed the city safely. By 2:30 A.M. Porter's entire fleet had made it except for one transport, which was sunk. The ships continued downriver for a rendezvous with Grant on the Louisiana shore south of Vicksburg.

The next day Grant sent his cavalry on a rampage through the territory east of Vicksburg, the Confederacy's heartland. He hoped to divert Pemberton's attention away from McClernand's and McPherson's corps moving south through Louisiana.

The hard-riding raid, led by Colonel Benjamin H. Grierson, a thirty-seven-year-old former music teacher, was a stunning success. The raiders not only traversed 476 miles in sixteen days, pillaging and fighting all the way, but they also preoccupied much of Pemberton's forces. Grierson estimated that at one time the Confederates had 20,000 men out searching for him. Grant later regarded the mission as "one of the most brilliant cavalry exploits of the war," and Grierson did not even like horses. One had kicked him in the head when he was a child.

As Grierson was leading Pemberton's infantry and

cavalry units on a wild chase through the state of Mississippi, the Union corps arrived at Hard Times, their destination. From there, Porter's squadrons of tinclads, wooden gunboats, flat-bottomed transports, supply craft, and skiffs were to ferry the soldiers across the river, but first they needed to capture the well-armed port on the other side, Grand Gulf.

With all movement by Union forces headed toward Grand Gulf, Pemberton began to suspect an attack there.

Grierson's raiders burning a Mississippi railroad station and tearing up tracks. *(Engraving courtesy of the Frank and Marie Wood Print Collection.)*

Grant launched yet another diversion. Porter's remaining boats transported Sherman's troops downstream to Snyder's Bluffs, northeast of Vicksburg, to fake an assault. Sherman's division paraded in front of the rebels over and over to make it appear as if there were many more Yanks than there were.

Just as Pemberton was about to send his army south to defend Grand Gulf, he received an urgent message from one of his brigadier generals: "The demonstration at Grand Gulf must be only a feint. Here is the real attack. The enemy are in front of me in force such as have never been seen before at Vicksburg. Send me reinforcements." Pemberton took the bait. By the time Pemberton redirected his troops toward Chickasaw Bayou, Sherman's pretend assault ended, and the real naval attack at Grand Gulf began.

Despite all their plots and diversions, the Yankees failed to take Grand Gulf. Confederate cannon perched high on cliffs above the river had the advantage over Porter's gunboats. The Union army could not be ferried across safely.

A freed slave told Grant there was a crossing nine miles south at Bruinsburg. The commander shifted his army downriver. Here is where Grant's schemes paid off.

Union gunboats attacking at Grand Gulf.

Pemberton had no more men to spare, and so he could not protect Bruinsburg. Grant's army crossed the river unopposed.

Grant experienced

a degree of relief scarcely ever equaled since. . . . I was now in the enemy's country, with a vast river

and the stronghold of Vicksburg between me and my base of supplies. But I was on dry ground on the same side of the river with the enemy. All the campaigns, labors, hardships, and exposures from the month of December previous to this time that had been made and endured were for the accomplishment of this one object.

In the meantime, without his father's permission, Grant's son, Fred, started an adventure of his own. He talked his way onto one of Porter's transports in the second group to run past Vicksburg's batteries. Although the boat he was on sank, he escaped and caught up with his father in Bruinsburg. But while Fred slept, Grant and his troops snuck off, leaving the boy in camp. Determined not to miss the action, Fred, wearing the sword and sash his father never used, started out on foot. He soon joined a detachment that was collecting the dead for burial. Sickened by the sights, he transferred to a division taking the wounded to a log-house hospital. "Here the scenes were so terrible that I became faint and ill, and making my way to a tree, sat down, the most woebegone twelve-year-old lad in America," Fred later recalled.

Commissioner Dana met up with Fred and together they headed off in search of Fred's father—and the impending battle. Astride two captured old plowhorses, one with a bridle made from an old clothesline, the pair of adventurers eventually reached Grant.

From Bruinsburg Grant's army moved on Port Gibson. The rebel forces retreated to Grand Gulf, which they evacuated on May 3, 1863.

When Grant realized that it would be a long delay before Banks could join him and that Johnston was trying to scrape together an army at Jackson, he made a bold decision. Rather than attack Vicksburg from the south, a more obvious route, he chose to move inland against Jackson, sever the city's communication and supply lines, and then attack from the east. This choice went directly against Sherman's advice, who warned that he would be placing his forces between two enemies, an incredible risk. But Grant believed his army could live off the land while disguising his real objective—Vicksburg. Everything was at stake—his military career, the campaign, and thousands of lives—yet the last few months' experience had given Grant a new confidence. Relying on his judgment and instincts alone, he now took total control of the campaign.

Grant drove his forces toward Jackson, Mississippi, an important manufacturing town for the Confederates. On the march the men in blue lived off what they collected from surrounding farms and plantations. The troops proved to be such good foragers that Fred Grant often preferred eating with the enlisted men rather than with his father because their food was better.

By mid-May 1863 many of the men lacked blankets and

Union troops destroying telegraph lines and buildings in the city of Jackson.

tents, and nearly a third marched barefoot. Commissioner Dana reported that Grant often slept on the ground, "without a tent, in the midst of his soldiers, with his saddle for a pillow and without even an overcoat for covering."

After a costly and bloody battle Grant conquered Jackson

and drove out Johnston's army. Sherman's bluecoats burned so many buildings they nicknamed the town "Chimneyville," for in many places that was all that was left.

Grant's rapid and unexpected movements divided and confused the Confederate commanders. President Jefferson

Davis ordered Pemberton to remain in Vicksburg and to hold it "at all costs." He assured Pemberton that relief would be sent if a siege developed. Johnston, though, was willing to sacrifice Vicksburg to attack Grant's army. He urged Pemberton to join forces with his 6,000 men to defeat Grant, even though that would leave the city undefended.

After calling a war council, Pemberton and his officers, ignoring both orders, decided to cut Grant's supply lines with a mobile force, while leaving some troops behind to defend the city. They did not know that Grant's troops were able to survive off the land and local farms.

On Sunday, May 16, Grant's infantry of 30,000 intercepted Pemberton's forces at a spot known as Champion's Hill. The hill was the highest point in the area and became the focus of the fiercest battle in the entire Vicksburg campaign. Whoever held the high ground was sure to win the battle.

Again and again the 22,000 Confederate soldiers on the hill repelled the Federals who were sent against them. The Federals fought no less valiantly. One Union sergeant commented on the mad fury that seemed to have gripped himself and his comrades: "Every human instinct is carried away by a torrent of passion, kill, kill, KILL, seems to fill your heart and be written over the face of all nature."

Suddenly the rebel defense collapsed. Panicked, the men in gray began rushing in all directions. Realizing that the battle was lost, Pemberton ordered a general retreat. As the Federals chased after the fleeing Confederates, a sharpshooter nicked young Fred Grant in the leg. When an officer asked the slightly injured boy what was wrong, he moaned, "I am killed."

In the end, 490 bodies, some dressed in blue, some in gray, littered Champion's Hill. Union casualties totaled 2,441 to the Confederate's 3,839. Union Brigadier General Alvin Hovey asked the few men gathered near his old regiment's flag, "Where are the rest of my boys?" A soldier, pointing to the hill, replied, "They are lying over there." Hovey rode away weeping. It had been a bloody battle and perhaps the most decisive of the entire campaign.

Pemberton took the defeat with a heavy heart. As he drove his forces back to defend Vicksburg, perhaps he suspected the campaign's eventual outcome. "Just thirty years ago," he said bitterly, "I began my . . . cadetship at the U.S. Military Academy. . . . Today—the same date—that career is ended in disaster and disgrace."

Yanks pursue retreating rebels at Champion's Hill, also known as the Battle of Baker Creek.

Grant had marched 200 miles in eighteen days and had fought five victorious battles. Pemberton, Johnston, and Davis stood divided both physically and strategically, and now at last Vicksburg lay ahead. Could the Confederate commanders come together in time to defeat Grant's army before it took the city?

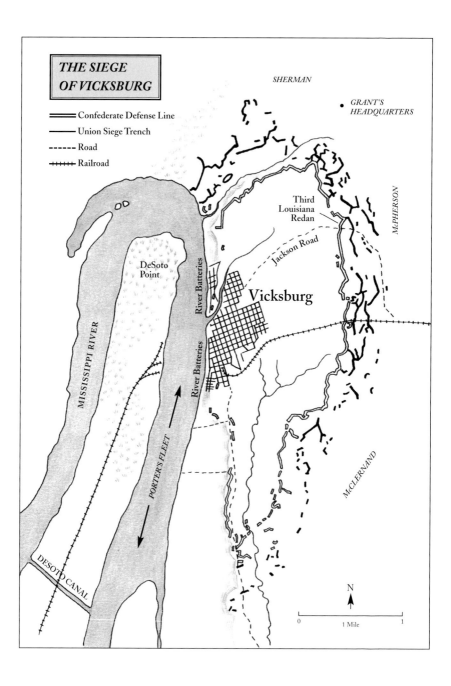

Johnny, Keep Your Head Down

For the citizens of Vicksburg, nothing was more dispiriting than seeing the hopeless Confederate troops returning. Said twenty-seven-year-old Mary Loughborough, "In all the dejected uncertainty, the stir of horsemen and wheels began. . . . Soon, straggler after straggler came by, then groups of soldiers worn and dusty with the long march."

Another Vicksburg resident, Dora Miller, who secretly supported the Union, described the scene: "Wan, hollow-eyed, ragged, footsore, bloody—the men limped along, unarmed but followed by siege-guns, ambulances, gun-carriages, and wagons in aimless confusion."

Pemberton now faced a difficult decision: either stay and defend the city as Davis ordered or fight his way out and join forces with Johnston. Which strategy would best serve the South? He called a war council, during which he and his officers voted unanimously against withdrawing. Pemberton responded to Johnston, "I still conceive it [Vicksburg] to be the most important point in the Confederacy."

Within forty-eight hours, the Confederates, now safe behind Vicksburg's elaborate fortifications, regained their confidence. Pemberton had six weeks' worth of food and ammunition in reserve and about 30,000 men, including 10,000 who had not served at Champion's Hill and were fresh and eager to fight. This army was smaller than Grant's 45,000, but the city's formidable defenses evened the odds.

Confederate Fortifications

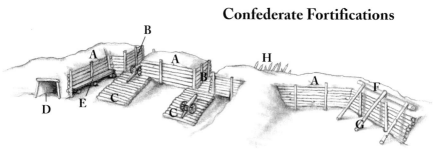

A. Parapet
B. Embrasure
C. Platform
D. Bombproof

E. Firing Step
F. Head Log
G. Crossbars, or Skids
H. Chevaux-de-frise

By May 19 most of Grant's divisions reached Vicksburg. The men were stunned by the enemy's defenses. Eight miles of fortifications wrapped around Vicksburg in a crescent. As one soldier put it: "Lines of heavy rifle-pits, surmounted with head logs, ran along the bluffs, connecting fort with fort, and filled with veteran infantry. . . . The approaches to this position were frightful—enough to appall the stoutest heart."

On the morning of Friday, May 22, hoping the rebel troops had lost their nerve to fight, Grant prepared to take Vicksburg by storm and ordered a direct assault. McClernand, who was determined to capture the glory for himself, attacked first.

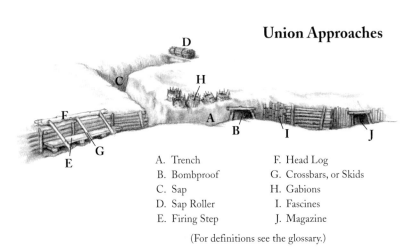

Union Approaches

A. Trench	F. Head Log
B. Bombproof	G. Crossbars, or Skids
C. Sap	H. Gabions
D. Sap Roller	I. Fascines
E. Firing Step	J. Magazine

(For definitions see the glossary.)

But the Confederate troops were not as demoralized as Grant hoped. Each time the Yanks charged toward the parapets, the rebels held their ground and showered them with lead. Here and there soldiers in blue mounted the barrier's ridge and planted their flags, but they could not advance or hold their positions.

At the climax of the battle one of Sherman's regiments ran out of ammunition. Orion R. Howe, a fourteen-year-old drummer boy, stepped forward. He volunteered to fetch a fresh supply. Bounding across the hillside through a torrent of grapeshot, musketballs, and miniés, he was wounded just before running into General Sherman. The general insisted he go to a hospital. The boy refused, saying he needed to get the ammunition. Sherman advised him not to worry, that he would see to it himself. In 1896 Howe became the youngest person to receive the Medal of Honor for his heroism on that day.

Several times McClernand sent Grant urgent dispatches claiming that he was breaking through Confeder-

From previous page: On the morning of May 22, 1863, "at exactly ten o'clock," reported a Northern war correspondent, "the whole Federal army was transformed into a monster serpent" as it made an assault upon the Confederate works. The attack failed, costing Grant's army more than 3,000 men. *(Engraving courtesy of the Frank and Marie Wood Print Collection.)*

ate defenses and needed support. Grant reluctantly
ordered a second round of attacks. One colonel refused to
face the enemy, saying, "No man can return from the
charge alive!" At last he obeyed, only to be killed in the
first volley.

The Civil War was a new kind of war. The invention of
guns that could shoot rapidly and accurately over a longer
distance changed the rules. Now a mass charge against a
well-positioned enemy was suicidal. Death tolls for short
battles climbed at a terrifying pace. At the end of the day,
3,200 Yanks had been killed, wounded, or lost compared
to the Confederacy's 500 casualties.

The assault gained no ground and yet was one of the
costliest in the entire war for the Union. Grant explained,
"General McClernand's dispatches misled me as to the
real state of the facts, and caused much of the loss. He is
entirely unfit for the position of corps commander, both
on the march and on the battlefield."

The first round of attacks marked the end of
McClernand's command and the beginning of a new
strategy. Grant later wrote, "I now determined upon a
regular siege—to 'out-camp the enemy.' . . . As long as
we could hold our position the enemy was limited in

supplies of food, men, and munitions of war to what they had on hand. These could not last."

For three days the dead and wounded of both sides littered the bloodstained ground. Pemberton asked for a two-and-a-half-hour truce so that they might be given aid or buried. Grant stalled, then finally agreed. Soldiers rose from the trenches and thronged the breastworks as the fallen victims were either buried where they fell or carried from the fields.

When the task was completed, the two armies found time to tell stories and jokes. Ephraim Anderson, an eighteen-year-old Missouri rebel, noted that among the opposing Missouri troops old friends, even relatives, met and talked of home: "I saw a young soldier of our command meet a brother, on half-way ground, from the Federal lines, where they sat on a log and conversed with one another."

One Union soldier, Sergeant Osborn Oldroyd, recalled the scene: "Here a group of four played cards—two Yanks and two Rebs. There, others were jumping, while everywhere blue and gray mingled in conversation over the scenes which had transpired since our visit to the neighborhood." He added, "From the remarks of some of the rebels, I judged that their supply of provisions was getting low, and that they had no source from which to draw more. We gave them from our own rations some fat meat, crackers, coffee, and so forth."

When the truce ended, the Union soldiers returned to their trenches, calling over their shoulders, "Johnny, keep your head down," and the sharpshooters resumed their work. The crack of their guns continued until dark.

Back in Washington, Lincoln delighted in news of Grant's progress. He wrote to one congressman, "Whether Gen. Grant shall not consummate the capture of Vicksburg, his campaign from the beginning of the month up to the 22nd day of it, is one of the most brilliant in the world."

When May turned to June, Grant realized the siege might be a long one and sent for additional troops. He had posted several divisions to keep an eye on Johnston, who was slowly gathering troops and supplies but still posed little threat. President Davis had little to spare.

On June 7, just a short distance above Vicksburg, the Confederates made a bold attack on the Federal outpost at Milliken's Bend. One regiment of whites and three regiments of newly recruited blacks, known as the African Brigade, staffed the post. Many Northerners had opposed the use of black regiments, arguing that they wouldn't fight.

Union troops unloading supplies from Federal ships on the banks of the Mississippi near Vicksburg.

As the rebels charged forward wielding flashing bayonets, the Federals engaged them in brutal hand-to-hand combat. They were determined to hold their ground. Just as the Confederates gained the upper hand, two of

Porter's gunboats arrived, forcing the rebel troops to retreat.

Of the 652 Union soldiers who died that day at Milliken's Bend, 566 were from the African Brigade. This was

Hand-to-hand combat at Milliken's Bend.

the second time black regiments saw action in the Civil War. One impressed captain stated, "I never saw a braver company of men in my life. Not one of them offered to leave his place until ordered to fall back. . . . They met death coolly, bravely."

Back in Vicksburg the Yankees dug twelve miles of trenches around the city, trapping the Confederates

between the river and their own earthworks. Each day the
men zigzagged closer and closer to the enemy lines. One
Union soldier wrote, "When entrenchments were safe and
finished, still others yet farther in advance were made, as if
by magic, in a single night. Other zigzag underground
saps and mines were made for explosion under forts. Every
day the regiments, foot by foot, yard by yard, approached

nearer the strongly armed rebel works. The soldiers got so they bored like gophers and beavers, with a spade in one hand and a gun in the other."

A volunteer nurse for the Union army described a daily source of encouragement and admiration for the troops:

A typical Union battery where some men manned the sharpshooter posts while others rested and talked.

Nearly every day . . . General Grant rode around the fiery line of the besieged city on his little black horse; and his son Fred, about thirteen years old, who acted as his orderly, followed about fifty feet to his rear. . . .

There was great anxiety for General Grant. . . .

Personally he was beloved by officers and men, but there were deeper reasons. His life was so important to the Union cause that his death would have been the greatest calamity that the army could have suffered.

For those trapped in Vicksburg there was neither rest nor relief from the constant shellfire and cannonade. Food and water were scarce, the days like steambaths. Yet the soldiers took it in stride with few complaints. One soldier in gray wrote, "The fighting is now carried on quite systematically . . . in the morning there seems to be time allowed for breakfast, when all at once the work of destruction is renewed. There is about an hour at noon and about the same at sunset. Taking these three intervals out, the work goes on just as regularly as on a well-regulated farm and the noise is not unlike the clearing up of new ground when much heavy timber is cut down."

Sometimes the soldiers bolstered themselves with humorous, often satirical songs. "Life on the Vicksburg Bluff" is such a song. It was written by rebel Private Dalsheimer and sung to the tune of "Life on the Ocean Wave," a familiar song of the time.

Life on the Vicksburg Bluff

A life on the Vicksburg bluff,
A home in the trenches deep,
Where we dodge Yank shells enough,
And our old pea bread won't keep.

On old Logan's beef I pine,
For there's fat on his bones no more;
Oh, give me some pork and brine,
And tuck from the Sutler's store.

The bullets may whistle by,
The terrible bombs come down;
But give me full rations, and I
Will stay in my hole in the ground.

A life on the Vicksburg bluff,
A home in the trenches deep,
Where we dodge Yank shells enough,
And our old pea bread won't keep.

Pemberton, his army, and the citizens of Vicksburg placed all hopes of relief on Johnston. The Vicksburg newspaper, which could now only be printed on pieces of

Many companies had mascots. Perhaps the most famous mascot was Old Abe, an eagle, of Company C, 8th Wisconsin. Six different bearers were shot from beneath him, yet Old Abe survived the war. *(Photo courtesy of Vicksburg Old Courthouse Museum.)*

wallpaper due to lack of paper, tried to bolster spirits with predictions: "The undaunted Johnston is at hand" and "Hold out a few days longer, and our lines will be opened, the enemy driven away, the siege raised." But as the weeks passed with no sign of deliverance from Johnston, hope dwindled. On June 10, a daring courier snuck through the Federal lines with an urgent message from Pemberton: "I am waiting most anxiously to know your intentions. . . . I shall endeavor to hold out as long as we have anything to eat." Johnston replied, "I am too weak to save Vicksburg."

The citizens of Vicksburg dealt with the hardships as well as they could. Emma Balfour wrote in her diary, "As I sat at my window I saw mortars from the west passing entirely over the house, and the parrot shells from the east passing by—crossing each other and this terrible fire raging in the center . . . I see we are to have no rest."

Many women and children sought shelter in caves

Caves dug into the hillsides were furnished with the necessities of daily life. Sometimes many people shared one cave.

Union troops dug bombproofs around a sympathizer's house to protect themselves from Confederate fire. *(Photo courtesy of Vicksburg Old Courthouse Museum.)*

hollowed out of Vicksburg's yellow clay hillsides. Men could be hired to dig them out at twenty to fifty dollars a cave. One woman gave birth to her son in a cave and named him Siege.

The women furnished their dirt dwellings with furniture and rugs in an effort to make them more comfortable. Cooking was done at the mouth of the cave and beds were toward the back. These snake-infested burrows offered minimal safety from enemy fire. Sometimes caves collapsed, trapping the people under many feet of soil.

Other Vicksburg residents remained in their homes, seeking shelter in their basements when the shells and mortars whizzed by too closely. One young bride, Dora Miller, complained to her diary, "We are utterly cut off from the world, surrounded by a circle of fire. . . . The fiery shower of shells goes on day and night. . . . People do nothing but eat what they can get, sleep when they can, and dodge the shells. . . . I think all the dogs and cats must be killed or starved. We don't see any more pitiful animals prowling around. . . . The confinement is dreadful."

About June 20, during one of the heaviest bombardments of the siege, Pemberton again begged Johnston for assistance: "My men have been thirty-four days in the trenches without relief, and the enemy within conversation distance. We are living on very reduced rations, and, as you know, are entirely isolated. What aid am I to expect from you?" Vicksburg's future now depended on whether Johnston would move against Grant before the Union starved out the Confederacy or broke through the city's fortifications.

Johnston refused to budge. He believed that it was suicidal for his ill-equipped force to attack Grant, whose position was strong and protected by powerful artillery. He needed more men and more equipment. Again he encouraged Pemberton's troops to fight their way out.

As opposing battle lines drew close to one another, Federal engineers were able to tunnel beneath the Third Louisiana Redan, a triangular fort guarding the main road into Vicksburg.

A Union correspondent described the actual explosion of June 25:

> At length all was in readiness. The fuse train was fired, and it went fizzing and popping through the zigzag line of trenches until . . . it vanished. Its disappearance was quickly succeeded by the explosion. . . . So terrible a spectacle is seldom witnessed. Dust, dirt, smoke, gabions, stockades, timber, gun-carriages, logs—in fact, everything connected with the fort—rose hundreds of feet into the air, as if vomited forth from a volcano. Some who were close spectators even say that they saw bodies of the poor wretches who a moment before had lined the ramparts of the work.

The Yankees set off powder under the Confederate earthworks, hoping to break through to the city.

Immediately following the explosion a column of Union troops charged into the crater it left. But the onslaught met with a fierce round of Confederate fire. The Yanks only succeeded in obtaining a brief hold on the crater before having to pull back and abandon their efforts in the area.

McPherson's saps approaching the Confederate defenses.

By June 28, 1863, as the two great armies in the east marched to meet their destinies at Gettysburg, the Confederate situation in Vicksburg grew desperate. Many of the soldiers were sick with dysentery and other diseases. They had been on nearly constant duty. They were short of ammunition and at the point of starvation. A communication was sent to Pemberton: "Our rations have been cut down to one biscuit and a small bit of bacon per day, not enough scarcely to keep soul and body together, much less to stand the hardships we are called upon to stand. If you can't feed us, you had better surrender us, horrible as the idea is. . . . This army is now ripe to mutiny unless it can be fed." It was signed, "Many soldiers."

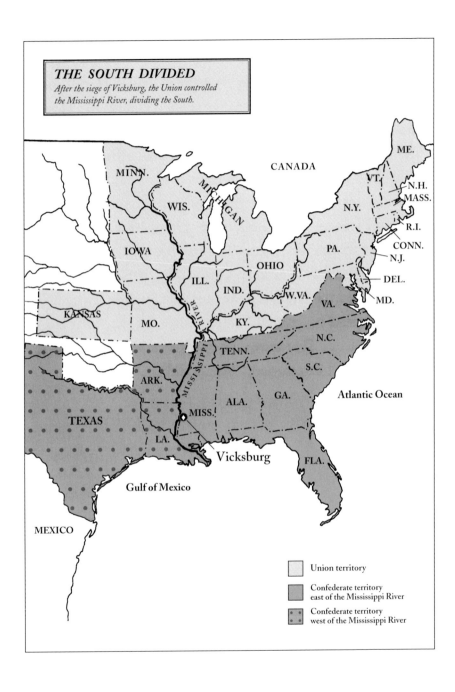

THE SOUTH DIVIDED

After the siege of Vicksburg, the Union controlled the Mississippi River, dividing the South.

CANADA

ME.

MINN.

VT.

N.H.

MASS.

WIS.

MICHIGAN

N.Y.

R.I.

IOWA

PA.

CONN.

N.J.

OHIO

DEL.

ILL.

IND.

W.VA.

MD.

KANSAS

MO.

MISSISSIPPI RIVER

KY.

VA.

N.C.

TENN.

S.C.

ARK.

ALA.

GA.

Atlantic Ocean

TEXAS

MISS.

LA.

Vicksburg

FLA.

Gulf of Mexico

MEXICO

Union territory

Confederate territory
east of the Mississippi River

Confederate territory
west of the Mississippi River

Vicksburg Has Surrendered

Time had run out for the city. Pemberton would not wait any longer for Johnston. On July 2 he called a war council and polled each officer: surrender or fight?

Much hinged on the vote. If they continued on, hundreds would perish from starvation and disease. If they surrendered, they were handing control of the Mississippi River over to the North and would lose their primary means of shipping and receiving much needed supplies.

At the conclusion of the vote Pemberton addressed those present:

> Well, gentlemen, I have heard your votes and I agree with your almost unanimous decision, though my own preference would be to put myself at the head of my troops and make a desperate effort to cut our way

through the enemy. . . . Far better would it be for me to die at the head of my army, even in a vain effort to force the enemy's lines, than to surrender it and live and meet the obloquy [abuse] which I know will be heaped upon me. But my duty is to sacrifice myself to save the army which has so nobly done its duty to defend Vicksburg. I therefore concur with you and shall offer to surrender.

On July 3, 1863, even as Confederate General Lee retreated from Gettysburg, Pemberton ordered the display of the white truce flags. He did not know that Johnston's army was finally on its way with plans to attack on July 7. Johnston had waited too long. Vicksburg was lost.

As the bleached banners rose along the parapets, hostilities ceased on both sides. A Confederate soldier described what happened next:

For forty-seven days we had been fighting. . . . Now the two armies stood up and gazed at each other with wondering eyes.

Winding around the hills—in ditches and parallels hitherto undreamed of by us—one long line

Grant and Pemberton met to determine the terms of surrender. Grant wanted Vicksburg, and not prisoners. He asked Pemberton to march his men out, have them give up their arms, and promise not to go back to the Confederate armies.

after another started into view, looking like huge blue snakes coiling around the ill-fated city. They were amazed at the paucity of our numbers; we were astonished at the vastness of theirs.

Grant and Pemberton met briefly on a hillside beside a bullet-riddled oak. They had served in the same division in the Mexican War. Grant greeted his enemy as an old acquaintance, but the Union commander's terms of unconditional surrender were sharply refused. Negotiations continued back and forth through the night.

At last, early in the morning of July 4, Independence Day, a brief note of submission arrived at Grant's headquarters. Fred Grant recounted his father's reaction: "He opened it, gave a sigh of relief, and said calmly, 'Vicksburg has surrendered.' I was thus the first to hear officially announced the news of the fall of the Gibraltar of America, and I ran out to spread the glad tidings. Officers rapidly assembled, and there was a general rejoicing."

Grant's army entering Vicksburg. Contrary to the sketch, news reports stated that most of Vicksburg's citizens stayed at home. *(Courtesy of Library of Congress.)*

Confiscated Confederate ammunition and artillery. *(Photo courtesy of Vicksburg Old Courthouse Museum.)*

To the people of Vicksburg the surrender was a crushing blow. They would not celebrate the Fourth of July again until the end of World War II.

As the Confederates paraded forward to surrender their arms and supplies, the Federal soldiers did not gloat as victors often do. A Confederate sergeant wrote, "No word of exultation was uttered to irritate the feelings of the prisoners. On the contrary, every sentinel who came upon post brought haversacks filled with provisions."

Another Confederate soldier, S. R. Martin, recalled, "Very shortly after the surrender, many of the [Yankee] boys began coming over to our lines to see us, and to observe us meet each other with cordial hand-shakes, it could hardly be realized that we had for days and weeks been engaged in killing each other without mercy."

The Union troops marched into the city and took 31,600 prisoners, 60,000 muskets, and 172 cannon. The very last casualty of the campaign occurred when a mishandled gun collected from a trench accidentally fired and killed a soldier in the act of surrendering.

The Union was victorious at Gettysburg, and on July 8, only four days after the capture of Vicksburg, discouraged Confederates surrendered Port Hudson. Meanwhile Sherman and his corps rode hard against Joe Johnston, driving him from Mississippi and destroying Confederate communications to the east.

When Colonel Josiah Gorgas, a respected Confederate leader, learned of Lee's and Pemberton's defeats he wrote in his diary,

> One brief month ago we were apparently at the point of success. Lee was in Pennsylvania, threatening Harrisburgh, and even Philadelphia. Vicksburgh seemed to laugh all Grant's efforts to scorn. . . . Now the picture is just as sombre as it

was bright then. Lee failed at Gettysburgh. . . .
Vicksburgh and Port Hudson capitulated, surrendering thirty-five thousand men and forty-five
thousand arms. It seems incredible that human
power could effect such a change in so brief a space.
Yesterday, we rode on the pinnacle of success—
today absolute ruin seems to be our portion. The
Confederacy totters to its destruction.

When President Lincoln received news of the Vicksburg victory, he was overjoyed. He wrote a letter to Grant,
whom he had never met, and admitted that throughout
the campaign he had doubted many of the major general's
decisions. But no more. He concluded by saying, "I now
wish to make a personal acknowledgment that you were
right and I was wrong."

Two great innovations came out of the Vicksburg campaign. The first was the discovery that a large army could
operate deep within enemy territory, cut off from its supply line. Sherman, who had initially opposed Grant's tac-
tic, put it to its greatest test when he marched through the
Deep South from 1864 to 1865.

The second innovation to have a major impact on the

Major General Ulysses S. Grant receiving his commission as lieutenant general from President Lincoln.

war's outcome was the Union's enlistment of black freemen and former slaves. The new supply of fighting men gave the Union a huge advantage over the Confederacy, whose fighting force was dwindling. By the end of the war, black soldiers made up one-tenth of the North's army.

Following his success at Vicksburg, Ulysses S. Grant was sent to Chattanooga where the Union army was under siege. Within weeks he broke the siege and drove off the enemy. This spectacular victory convinced Lincoln that Grant was the man who could win the war. In March 1864, Grant became general in chief. He led the Army of the Potomac against Richmond, forcing

General Robert E. Lee to surrender at Appomattox on April 9, 1865. The Civil War was over.

Grant became president of the United States in 1869, but his administration was tormented by political and financial scandals. After leaving office, his personal reputation still intact, he succeeded in writing his *Personal Memoirs*. He died from throat cancer at the age of sixty-three, just four days after its completion.

Only two months after the surrender of Vicksburg, Sherman and his family boarded a transport to leave for Memphis. Sherman noticed that his oldest boy, nine-year-old Willy, was feverish. Willy died of typhoid a few days later. Sherman was grief-stricken, but his anguish did not keep him from his duties. Within the year, he began his famous March to the Sea, during which he burned Atlanta and left a path of destruction in his wake.

When the war ended, Sherman refused all requests to run for president, saying he'd rather spend four years in prison than in the White House. When he died of pneumonia in 1891, Joe Johnston, his Civil War adversary, attended his funeral and refused to wear a hat out of respect for his late-in-life friend. Johnston caught pneumonia standing in the cold winter air and died shortly afterward.

John Pemberton received all the criticism he expected. He finished out the war and retired to a war-ravaged farm. The farm failed. He died in 1881 and is still remembered as the general who lost Vicksburg.

The surrender of Vicksburg and the simultaneous rebuff at Gettysburg of Lee's invasion into the North gave the Union the advantage for the first time in the war.

Of the two victories, though, Vicksburg was the one that set the stage for the South's ultimate defeat. After two years of land and naval warfare, the South was split, its flow of supplies and ammunition was severed, its momentum checked. The Federal army and navy

A memorial to Lieutenant General John C. Pemberton stands today in the Vicksburg National Military Park.

could now conduct more successful maneuvers, and merchants and farmers in the North regained their prewar trade routes.

At last the key was in the Union's pocket. The entire Mississippi River was under the North's control, and in the words of Lincoln, "The Father of the Waters again goes unvexed to the sea."

Vicksburg National Cemetery.

Notes

Vicksburg Is the Key

3   Lincoln's comment regarding Vicksburg as the key comes from several sources, including Wheeler's *The Siege of Vicksburg*, page 1, and Hoehling's *Vicksburg: 47 Days of Siege*, page 1.

3   Lincoln's explanation is in Martin's *Vicksburg Campaign*, page 11.

5   Jefferson Davis's statement comes from Korn's *War on the Mississippi*, page 16.

8   The two quotes in the photo caption are from Catton's *Grant Takes Command*, pages 159 and 160, respectively.

9   Lincoln's response to calls for Grant's dismissal is from *Battle Cry of Freedom* by McPherson, page 4, and *Vicksburg* by Hoehling, page 3.

9–10   The engineer's description of Vicksburg was found in Ballard's *Campaign for Vicksburg*, page 2.

The Yankees Are Coming!

13, 15   Grant's opinion of McClernand and his comments about obtaining supplies come from his *Personal Memoirs*, pages 253 and 258, respectively.

17, 18, 19   The telegraph message, the description of the battle at Chickasaw Bayou, and Sherman's letter to his wife are all from Korn's *War on the Mississippi*, pages 63–64 and 68.

21, 23   Grant's description of the winter comes from his *Personal Memoirs*, page 270.

26   The comment regarding Albert Cashier is taken from Robertson's *Tenting Tonight*, page 27.

29   General Cadwallader's opinion of Grant is taken from *Battle Cry of Freedom* by McPherson, page 588.

On Dry Ground with the Enemy

32, 34, 35, 37, 38   Grant's remark from his *Personal Memoirs* is quoted in McPherson's *Battle Cry of Freedom*, page 627. Colonel Vilas's observation is from Wheeler's *The Siege of Vicksburg*, pages 98–99, as are Charles Dana's evaluation of Grant, page 99; the reporter's account of Porter's plan, page 106; General Maury's impressions, page 108; and Mary Loughborough's description of the fleet's passing (from her book *My Cave Life at Vicksburg*), page 110.

38–39   Frederick Grant's description of the campaign is in Hankinson's *Vicksburg 1863*, pages 37–38.

39, 41   Grant's remark regarding Grierson's raid and the urgent message to Pemberton both come from *War on the Mississippi* by Korn, pages 96–97.

42–43   Grant's feelings following his crossing at Bruinsburg were first expressed in his *Personal Memoirs*, page 284.

44   Fred Grant's experiences were quoted in Wheeler's *The Siege of Vicksburg*, page 126.

46   Dana's report was found in Korn's *War on the Mississippi*, page 109.

48   Davis's orders to Pemberton come from Martin's *The Vicksburg Campaign*, page 120.

48–49   The Union sergeant's description of the battle at Champion's Hill is from Korn's *War on the Mississippi*, page 119.

49   Young Fred Grant's response to his injury is found in Wheeler's *The Siege of Vicksburg,* page 158.

49   Hovey's query and the answer are found in *War on the Mississippi* by Korn, page 122.

49   Pemberton's statement about his career is quoted in Wheeler's *The Siege of Vicksburg,* page 158.

Johnny, Keep Your Head Down

53   Mary Loughborough's impression of returning soldiers is from her book *My Cave Life in Vicksburg,* page 42.

53   Dora Miller's impression of the same was given in Wheeler's *The Siege of Vicksburg,* page 160.

54, 55,   Pemberton's response to Johnson, the soldier's description
59   of Vicksburg's defenses, the colonel's refusal to advance, and Grant's explanation regarding McClernand's dispatches all come from Martin's *The Vicksburg Campaign,* pages 122, 127, and 129.

58   The correspondent's account of the May 22 assault in the caption comes from Cotton's *Vicksburg: Southern Stories of the Siege,* page 22.

59–60   Grant's plan to use a siege appeared in his *Personal Memoirs,* page 312.

60   Ephraim Anderson's observations appeared in Cotton's *Vicksburg: Southern Stories of the Siege,* page 26.

60–61   Sergeant Oldroyd's statement is quoted in Wheeler's *The Siege of Vicksburg,* pages 176 and 177.

61   "Johnnie, keep heads down after daylight" was found in an article by J. H. Jones, *The Rank and File of Vicksburg,* in volume VII of a publication by the Mississippi Historical Society, edited by Frank L. Riley.

61 Lincoln's words written to a congressman come from Hankinson's *Vicksburg 1863*, page 69.

64 The captain's comments regarding the black soldiers at Milliken's Bend come from Mettger's *Till Victory Is Won*, page 62.

65–66 The soldier's description of Union approaches to enemy lines was found in Martin's *The Vicksburg Campaign*, pages 139–40.

67–68 The nurse's words regarding Grant come from Wheeler's *The Siege of Vicksburg*, page 186.

68 The Confederate soldier's statement is from Hankinson's *Vicksburg 1863*, page 72.

70 The newspaper predictions are from McPherson's *Battle Cry of Freedom*, page 634.

70 Pemberton's message and Johnson's response appeared in Cotton's *Vicksburg: Southern Stories of the Siege*, page 43.

71 Emma Balfour's diary entry for June 2 appears in her published diary titled *Vicksburg: A City Under Siege*.

73 Dora Miller's statement was quoted in Hoeling's *Vicksburg*, page 40.

74 The correspondent's description of the June 25 explosion appears in Wheeler's *Voices of the Civil War*, page 345.

77 The communication to Pemberton appears in Wheeler's *The Siege of Vicksburg*, page 224.

Vicksburg Has Surrendered

79–80, 80–81 Pemberton's speech at the July 2 war council as noted by Confederate engineer Samuel Lockett and the Confederate soldier's description of the truce come from Wheeler's *The Siege of Vicksburg*, pages 229–30 and 230–31, respectively.

82, 83   Fred Grant's account of the surrender and the Confederate sergeant's account are both from Wheeler's *The Siege of Vicksburg*, pages 232 and 233, respectively.

83–84   S. R. Martin's remembrance of the surrender is recounted in his personal papers in the Vicksburg Old Courthouse Museum collection.

84–85   Colonel Gorgas's diary entry comes from McPherson's *Battle Cry of Freedom*, page 665.

85   Lincoln's letter to Grant was found in Korn's *War on the Mississippi*, page 159.

89   Lincoln's response to the capture of Vicksburg appears in McPherson's *Battle Cry of Freedom*, page 638.

Glossary

battery. A placement of guns or heavy artillery.

bayonet. A knife attached to the muzzle end of a gun, used in close combat.

bombproof. A bomb shelter.

breastwork. A quickly built and temporary defense structure.

cannonade. To bombard with cannon fire.

chevaux-de-frise. Sharpened stakes used to obstruct an enemy attack.

corduroy. To build a road by laying logs side by side.

crossbars (skids). Poles that keep the head log from falling into the trench if hit by artillery fire.

embrasure. Opening in parapet from which to fire cannon.

fascine. Bundle of cane to brace sides of trench.

firing step. Platform on which sharpshooters stood to shoot.

fort. A fortified position for troops; can be surrounded by a mound of earth called a rampart.

gabion. Basket of cane and vines filled with earth and stone used as a barricade against explosives and artillery fire.

grapeshot. A cluster of small iron balls fired from a cannon.

haversack. A one-strapped bag worn over the shoulder to haul supplies while on the march.

head log. Protection for sharpshooters from enemy musket fire.

hurricane deck. The upper deck on a passenger steamship.

ironclad. A warship having sides armored with metal sheets.

levee. An embankment raised to prevent a river from overflowing.

magazine. A place where ammunition is stored.

minié ball. A new type of ammunition that was more accurate, harder hitting, and loaded more quickly than older types.

mortar. A muzzle-loading cannon that fires shells at low speeds and at a sharp angle.

musketball. A metal ball shot from a smoothbore shoulder gun.

orderly. A soldier assigned to serve a superior officer and carry orders and messages.

parapet. Wall of earth and log to protect soldiers from enemy fire.

pea bread. A mixture of ground peas used in place of cornmeal.

picket. A detachment of one or more soldiers sent ahead as a lookout.

platform. Supports artillery; guns are pushed forward on the platform for firing at the enemy and are rolled back for reloading.

ration. A fixed portion of food distributed to each soldier.

redan. A triangular earthen fort.

redoubt. A rectangular earthen fort.

sap. A narrow trench dug for protection while approaching location under enemy fire.

sap roller. A fortification made of cane and vine and packed with dirt and cotton to protect engineers and fatigue party (sappers).

siege. The surrounding and blockading of a city or fortress with the intent to capture it or force it to surrender.

supply line. The means by which necessities are provided to troops in the field.

tinclad. Light river craft with armor plating less than an inch thick; true ironclads had more than a hundred tons of plating bolted to the wooden hulls.

trench. A hole dug into the earth to enable soldiers to stand erect without exposure to enemy fire.

volley. The simultaneous firing of a number of weapons.

Bibliography

Ballard, Michael B. *The Campaign for Vicksburg.* Conshohocken, PA: Eastern National Park and Mountain Assoc., 1996.

Bowman, John S. *The Civil War: Day by Day.* Greenwich, CT: Brompton Books Corp., 1989.

Catton, Bruce. *Grant Takes Command.* Boston: Little, Brown, 1968.

Cotton, Gordon. *Vicksburg: Southern Stories of the Siege.* Vicksburg: Cotton, 1988.

————. *Yankee Bullets, Rebel Rations: Caught Between Two Armies, Citizens of Vicksburg Recall the Horrors of the 1863 Siege.* Vicksburg: Cotton, 1989.

Davis, Kenneth C. *Don't Know Much About the Civil War: Everything You Need to Know About America's Greatest Conflict but Never Learned.* New York: Avon Books, 1996.

Foote, Shelby. *The Civil War: A Narrative.* New York: Random House, 1963.

Freedman, Russell. *Lincoln: A Photobiography.* New York: Clarion Books, 1987.

Gay, Kathlyn, and Martin Gay. *Civil War.* New York: Twenty-First Century Books, 1995.

Grant, Ulysses S. *Personal Memoirs of U.S. Grant.* New York: Thomas Y. Crowell Co., 1894.

Hankinson, Alan. *Vicksburg 1863: Grant Clears the Mississippi.* London: Osprey Military Publishing Co., 1993.

Hoehling, A. A. *Vicksburg: 47 Days of Siege.* Mechanicsburg, PA: Army Times Publishing Co., 1969.

Korn, Jerry. *War on the Mississippi: Grant's Vicksburg Campaign.* Alexandria, VA: Time-Life Books, 1985.

Loughborough, Mary. *My Cave Life at Vicksburg.* New York: D. Appleton & Co., 1864.

Martin, David. *The Vicksburg Campaign.* Conshohocken, PA: Combined Books, 1990.

McFeeley, William S. *Grant: A Biography.* New York: W.W. Norton, 1981.

McPherson, James. *Battle Cry of Freedom: The Civil War Era.* New York: Oxford University Press, 1988.

Mettger, Zak. *Till Victory Is Won: Black Soldiers in the Civil War.* New York: Lodestar Books, 1994.

Murphy, Jim. *The Boys' War: Confederate and Union Soldiers Talk About the Civil War.* New York: Clarion Books, 1990.

Ray, Delia. *Behind the Blue and the Gray: The Soldier's Life in the Civil War.* New York: Lodestar Books, 1991.

Robertson, James I. *Tenting Tonight: The Soldier's Life.* Alexandria, VA: Time-Life Books, 1984.

Sherman, William T. *Memoirs of General William T. Sherman.* New York: Library of America, 1990.

Stern, Philip Van Doren. *Secret Missions of the Civil War.* New York: Wings Books, 1959.

Wheeler, Richard. *The Siege of Vicksburg.* New York: Thomas Y. Crowell Co., 1978.

———. *Voices of the Civil War.* New York: Meridian, 1976.

Internet Sites

There are many helpful internet sites. To learn more about Vicksburg, consult the Vicksburg National Military Park site at **http://www.nps.gov/vick/home.htm**.

Some other sites relating to the Civil War that also provide links include the following:

- Library of Congress Civil War Photograph Archive
  http://rs6.loc.gov/cwphome.html
- The American Civil War Home Page
  http://sunsite.utk.edu/civil_war
- U.S. Civil War Center
  http://www.cwc.lsu.edu
- The Civil War Revisited: Resources on the Web
  http://www.techstop.com/~deb/cw/cw_links.html

Index

Italic page numbers refer to captions and illustrations.

African Brigade, 61–64
Anderson, Ephraim, 60
Appomattox, 87
Arkansas, 4
Army of the Potomac, 86–87
Atlanta, 87

Baker Creek. *See* Champion's Hill
Balfour, Emma, 71
Balfour, William and Emma, home, 16–17, 18
Banks, Gen. Nathaniel, 31, 45
bayous, 23, *27*
black soldiers, 21, *22,* 61–64, *64–65,* 86
Bruinsburg, 41–42, 44

Cashier, Albert, 26
Champion's Hill, 48–49, *50,* 54
Chattanooga, 86

Chickasaw Bayou, 14, *17,* 18, 41
cities, attacks on, 15–16
Civil War
new technologies used in, 16, 59
and slavery issue, 6–7, 19–20
Confederacy (South), 3–4, 5, 6, 88
corduroying, 33, *33*
cotton, 4, 5

Dalsheimer, Private, 68
Dana, Charles, 33–34, 44, 46
Davis, Jefferson, 5, 10, 11, 47–48, 51, 53, 61
Department of the Tennessee, 9
DeSoto Canal, 21–23, *22,* 28
DeSoto Point, 17, 21, *22,* 35

Ellet, Col. Charles Rivers, 24, 25
Emancipation Proclamation, 19–20, *20*

Fall, Philip H., 17–18
Farragut, Adm. David, 4
Fort DeRussy, 25
Fort Donelson, 7
Fort Henry, 7
Fort Pemberton, 27
4th Iowa Division, 18–19

Gettysburg, 77, 80, 84, 85, 88
Gorgas, Col. Josiah, 84–85
Grand Gulf, 31, 40, 41, *42–43*, 44
Grant, Frederick Dent, 35, *38*, 38–39, 44, 45, 49, 67, 82
Grant, Julia, 35, *38*
Grant, Maj. Gen. Ulysses S., 7–9, *8*, 13–15, 16, 20–24, 26, 28–29, 31–32, 33–35, *38*, 38–39, 41–45, 46–47, 48, 51, 54, 55, 58–60, *58*, 61, 67–68, 73, 74, *81*, 81–82, *82*, 84, 85, *86*
    reputation and character of, 7–9, *8*, 32, 34
    and Sherman, *8*, 14, *15*, 32
    after Vicksburg, 86–87

winter "experiments," *12*, 21–28
Grierson, Col. Benjamin H., 39–40, *40*

Halleck, Maj. Gen. Henry, 9, 13
Hard Times, 40
Hodgers, Jennie, 26
Hovey, Brig. Gen. Alvin, 49
Howe, Orion R., 58

Illinois, 4
Indianola 25, *25*, 26

Jackson, Mississippi, 45, 46–47, *46–47*
Johnston, Gen. Joseph E. (Joe), 11, *11*, 35, 45, 47, 48, 51, 53, 54, 61, 69–70, 73–74, 79, 80, 84, 87

Lake Providence, 23, 28
Lee, Gen. Robert E., 32, 80, 84, 85, 87, 88
"Life on the Vicksburg Bluff," 68–69

Lincoln, Abraham, 3, 6, *6,* 7, 9, 13, 19–20, *20,* 21, 61, 85, *86,* 89

Loughborough, Mary, 37–38, 53

Louisiana, 4

McClernand, Maj. Gen. John, 13, *13,* 20, 32, 35, 39, 55, 58, 59

McPherson, Maj. Gen. James B., 20, 23, 32, 39, *76*

Martin, S. R., 83–84

Maury, Gen. Dabney, 36–37

Medal of Honor, 58

Miller, Dora, 53, 73

Milliken's Bend, 61–64, *64–65*

Mississippi, 5

Mississippi River ("Father of the Waters"), 3–4, 5, 79, 89

Morse, Samuel, 16

New Orleans, 4, *34*

Old Abe (mascot), *70*

Oldroyd, Sgt. Osborn, 60–61

Olds, Capt. William, 18

Pemberton, Lt. Gen. John C., *10,* 10–11, 16, 27, 35, 39–40, 41, 42, 48, 49, 51, 53–54, 60, 69, 70, 73, 74, 77, 79–80, 81, *81,* 84, 88, *88*

Porter, Adm. David Dixon, 16, 25, *25,* 26, 28, 31, 32, 33, 34, *34,* 35, 39, 40, 41, 44, 63

Port Gibson, 44

Port Hudson, 31, 84, 85

Queen of the West, 24, 24–25

Red River campaign, 24–26

Richmond, Virginia, 3, 86–87

Sherman, Maj. Gen. William Tecumseh, *8,* 14, *15,* 16, *17,* 18, 19, 20, 28, 32, 41, 45, 47, 58, 84, 85, 87

Sherman, Willy, 87

Shiloh, 9

slavery issue, 6–7, 19–20

Snyder's Bluffs, 41

Southern Rail Road of Mississippi, 5

Steele's Bayou expedition, 28
supply lines, 14–15, 16

telegraph, 16, 18
Texas, 4
Third Louisiana Redan, 74

Union (North), 3, 4, 6–7, 19–
   20, 88–89

Vick, Rev. Newit, 5
Vicksburg
   cave refuges in hillsides of,
      71, 71–73
   citizens of, 5, 53, 69–70,
      71–73, *82,* 83
   defense and fortification of,
      5, 9–11, 54, *54,* 55
   Grant's approach to, 9–10,
      30, 31–51
   military innovations in cam-
      paign against, 85–86

naval bombardment of
   (1862), 5–6, 7
naval runs past batteries of,
   31, 32, 34–39, *36–37,* 44
siege of, *52,* 53–77, *56–57,*
   62–63, 66–67
strategic importance of, 3–5,
   7, 53–54
surrender of, 79–84, *81, 82,*
   85, 87, 88
Vicksburg National Cemetery,
   89
Vilas, Col. William F., 32
Von Phul, 35, 38

Washburn, Gen. Cadwallader,
   29
women soldiers and spies, 26

Yazoo Pass project, 27, 28